Titles in the series:

DELETE
TIM COLLINS

IN THE STARS
ECHO FREER

KEEPER
ANN EVANS

KILL ORDER
DANIEL BLYTHE

LAST YEAR
IAIN McLAUGHLIN

PARADISE
TIM COLLINS

S/HE
CATHERINE BRUTON

THE CRAVING
CLIFF McNISH

Badger Publishing Limited, Oldmedow Road, Hardwick Industrial Estate, King's Lynn PE30 4JJ

Telephone: 01438 791037

www.badgerlearning.co.uk

LAST YEAR

IAIN McLAUGHLIN

Last Year ISBN 978-1-78464-712-4

Text © Iain McLaughlin 2017
Complete work © Badger Publishing Limited 2017

Publisher: Susan Ross
Senior Editor: Danny Pearson
Copyediting: Cambridge Publishing Management Ltd
Designer: Bigtop Design Ltd
Cover: Blend Images / Alamy

2 4 6 8 10 9 7 5 3 1

1 January

Mum gave me a diary for Christmas. What do I need a diary for? There's no way I will write my secrets in it. At least I've written on one page now so I don't need to feel guilty.

4 January

Back to college tomorrow? Already? How did that happen? Where did the holidays go?

5 January

Got the results of the exams we did before Christmas. Guess who got a top pass in all four exams? Me! Claire Mason.

I am a legend.

Official!

10 January

Mum's been feeling bad over the holidays. She's going to the doctor's in the morning. That means

she can't drive me to college. I have to get the bus.
That means getting up half an hour early. Ugh.

11 January

Mum saw her doctor. He gave her antibiotics
and took blood. They'll test it and tell her what's
wrong next week. She'll probably be better by the
time they tell her what was wrong. The bus was
horrible. It was raining and the bus smelled like
a wet dog. I had to sit in my classes with wet feet.
Spare socks and trainers are going to college with
me tomorrow just in case.

13 January

I felt guilty last night when I realised I hadn't
written anything in the diary. Am I addicted to
my diary already?

14 January

Today was rubbish.

That is all.

15 January

I should say why yesterday was rubbish. We're changing tutor for maths. Miss Afzal got promoted. Pity. I like her. Mum said I should just focus on my exams.

16 January

Mum's was a weird mood today. She was really grumpy and bad-tempered. She was late home from work tonight. It must have been a tough day.

22 January

I haven't written in the diary for nearly a week. Mum told me why she was so down. She got the results of her blood tests. She has cancer. She told me it's nothing to worry about. She said there's treatment she can get. She's going to be fine. She said so.

23 January

Why am I even looking at this diary? Being with Mum is more important.

25 January

I went to the hospital with Mum today. The doctors told us that the treatment will make her feel bad. We saw some of the other patients getting treatment – chemotherapy they call it. Two of them threw up. I think it was when Mum saw a woman with a bald head that it really got to her. She's terrified that she will lose her hair. I'm terrified I will lose my mum.

31 January

Mum had her first treatment today. She didn't feel too bad after it. I wanted to go with her but she said no. She doesn't want this to be a big deal. She doesn't want it to change my routine either.

3 February

Mum seems to have more energy. The doctors have given her steroids to keep her strength up. She laughed about it and said it would stop her being in the Olympics. She doesn't even watch sport! I wonder if it's an act to stop me from worrying. It's not working.

5 February

Today was normal. Mum went to work, dropped me off at college. I did my classes, met with my tutor, had lunch with friends. I didn't tell any of them about Mum being ill. I don't want them to look at me any differently than they do now. I wanted a normal day. That's what I got.

6 February

Today I wrote 3,000 words about a classic book for college. *Pride and Prejudice*. It's a brilliant book. I'm glad I actually read it and didn't cheat by watching it on Netflix. Mum is a book collector so I borrowed her copy. She takes a book with her when she goes to hospital.

11 February

I'm going to see that new superhero film tonight. With David Brady. The totally fit David Brady. It's not just us, but he asked me to go with a bunch from college. It doesn't feel right to have fun while Mum is ill but she told me to go. I'll make sure she is OK before I go and I won't stay out late.

12 February

(Just after midnight so it's the 12th).

The film was rubbish. I don't care. I had fun. David likes me. Mum was fine when I got home. She fell asleep watching TV.

13 February

I saw David at college today. We're going to do some studying together tomorrow. He has a lot of exams coming, too.

14 February

Does four hours of studying in the library count as a hot date on Valentine's Day? David bought me a cupcake with a heart on it. Maybe it was just a bribe to get me to do his studying for him?

15 February

Mum saw David when she dropped me at college this morning. She said he looks 'nice'. Is that good or bad?

18 February

I had to call an ambulance for Mum today. Her pills made her dizzy and she threw up everywhere. They kept her in hospital tonight. I cleaned up the sick when I got home.

19 February

Just home from the hospital. Mum's still there. She looks better but she's tired. She actually slept most of the time I was there. I just kept her company and studied. I got plenty of work done. It was really quiet. I was able to read in peace.

20 February

Mum is home. She's still tired but she's glad to be home. She wanted to start making tonight's tea as soon as we got home. No chance. I'm doing the cooking for a few days. So, we'll probably both be back in hospital with food poisoning soon!

21 February

I'm taking the day off from college to look after Mum. She is not happy about that. In fact, she's very angry. Too bad. I'm not leaving her.

22 February

Mum was stronger today so I went back to college. I saw David and apologised for not getting in touch. I told him Mum had been ill but I didn't say what was wrong. He was pretty nice about it.

24 February

I have to get an essay in by the 28th. I haven't even started it yet. I have a couple of late nights ahead.

27 February

Most of the essay is done. I had to help Mum a bit today, though. She's really tired. The steroids

have made her put on weight. It's getting
her down.

3 March

Another rough day with Mum. The doctors said
that the treatment would give her difficult days.
She can't sleep because she has aches and pains,
so she's tired and grumpy. I made her a sandwich
for lunch but she couldn't eat it - she has mouth
ulcers and they hurt too much. She said things
taste different too. She said she was sorry for
moaning so much.

5 March

Got my essay back. Normally I would have been
disappointed with the mark. With all the stuff that
has happened, I think it's OK. It's a pass anyway.

6 March

Had lunch with David. He thought I was avoiding
him. I told him it was just because Mum is ill. I
didn't mention cancer. I just said she needed to be
looked after for a while. I think he understands.

9 March

Better day. Mum got new pills a few days ago. These don't make her feel sick all the time. The mouth ulcers have mostly gone so she can eat again, too. She's in a better mood. She's going to tell Aunt Fiona about the cancer tonight.

10 March

Mum told Aunt Fiona last night. It was a big relief for her to actually tell somebody. Her boss knows, but he has to know because she is off work getting treatment twice a week. He is being pretty good about it. I think he fancies her. Aunt Fiona is cool. She was annoyed that Mum didn't tell her sooner, but just kept asking what she could do to help. I left the room so they could talk privately. I Snapchatted with David and told him what's wrong with Mum.

12 March

I got home from college tonight… and Aunt Fiona is here. She drove down from Edinburgh to

be with Mum. Mum's really glad to see her.
So am I.

16 March

I'm really glad Aunt Fiona is here. Mum has started to lose her hair. The chemotherapy made it look dull and lifeless. Now it's just falling out. She was doing so well. This is a big setback for her. I wish Aunt Fiona could stay but she can't. She has to go back to Edinburgh soon.

17 March

Aunt Fiona took Mum out for a drive today. It's still pretty cold so Mum wore a hat. It hid that she's losing her hair. I don't know what they talked about but they had serious faces on when they came back.

21 March

I missed the deadline for an essay today. I totally forgot about it until I got an email asking where it was. I feel like an idiot. I'm going to see my tutor tomorrow.

22 March

I met my tutor today. Aunt Fiona came along for support. Miss Afzal sat in on the meeting. She saw us coming in and said hello. When we explained why I was there she came in with us. She made sure I got an extension on the date for my essay. She even gave me a hug after the meeting. I don't think she's supposed to do that. I'm glad she did.

23 March

Aunt Fiona took Mum to the hospital today. I got ¾ of the essay done while they were gone. Mum came back with a full head of hair. She has a wig. She really wanted me to like it so I said it looks great.

25 March

Aunt Fiona went home today. She told me to phone her if it got too much. When she was here I felt like I could breathe. It felt like it wasn't up to me to deal with everything. I'm scared now that I'll let Mum down.

26 March

Handed my essay in at college today. It's not the best work ever, but it's OK.

27 March

Met David for coffee. He asked what I was doing next year. I haven't got a clue.

1 April

I was supposed to go to a comedy gig with David. Mum's nose started bleeding. She got really upset because it wouldn't stop. I couldn't leave her so I cancelled on the comedy.

2 April

Mum's nose seems OK now. David was fine about the comedy last night.

5 April

I think the hoover is now part of my arm. Mum doesn't have the strength to clean the house so I do it. She feels bad about it. It's not her fault.

7 April

I don't have to go to college now until my exams. I'm on revision break. This will sound horrible: I sort of need college – it gets me away from Mum's illness. It gives me a few hours every day when I can think of something else. That sounds so selfish.

11 April

Revision is going OK. Mum is tired. Chemotherapy leaves her worn out. She's had more nosebleeds. Her gums have been bleeding too. She's also had trouble going to the toilet. She's embarrassed by all of it. She keeps nagging me to study more.

13 April

David asked if I want to study with him tomorrow. We swap messages every day. I told him I need to stay with Mum… then I asked him to come over tomorrow and study here. He said yes but he won't come.

14 April

David did come. We studied for a few hours and talked rubbish in my room for another couple of hours. He's coming back tomorrow.

15 April

More studying, more tidying. Mum tired.

27 April

I have ignored you, diary. It's nothing personal. I've just been busy. I'm studying every day, cooking every day and cleaning most days. Mum is weak. I'm glad tomorrow is the last day of her chemotherapy. She's so weak. It's not just physical. She looks like she's tired of fighting this illness.

28 April

Mum's finished her treatment. We go back to the hospital next week for some tests. She's fed up of hospitals.

29 April

I just realised that the first exam is next week. I'm not ready. I haven't studied enough.

4 May

I had my first exam today. I wasn't ready for it. I did my best but I'm not confident. Everybody thought it was hard, but I really wasn't prepared.

5 May

Mum had some tests done today. I hit the books while they did them. Mum wanted the tests so that she could be told she'll be OK, but she's scared the results will say she's still sick. She tells me to be positive about my exams. I tell her to be positive about her tests.

11 May

Second exam today. It was English. I think I did pretty well. Reading Mum's books was a big help. I'm more confident about this one. That probably means I've failed it really badly.

12 May

Best day ever. Mum got her results back. There's no sign of cancer. She has to keep going back to get checked, but right now they can't find any cancer. Mum is so relieved. She cried for half an hour when they told us. I'm so happy.

14 May

Maths exam today. I think I did well on this one. Today I can do anything.

21 May

Last exam. I did OK. I don't know if I've done enough to make it to university. If I haven't I'll make it up next year. I'm happy anyway.

23 May

Went to see a film with David. Mum threw me out for the afternoon and told me to have fun. We went for chips with curry sauce. Romantic or what?

28 May

Mum is a maniac. After everything she's been through, she wants to go back to work full-time next week.

30 May

Mum's boss told her she can start work in two weeks – but she can only work part-time for a month. They call it a 'phased return'. Why do people need to give things fancy titles?

12 June

Diary, sorry I'm not writing in you much. I'm just busy. Mum is getting stronger. Her hair is growing. She still wears her wig, but her own hair is coming back. She looks more like herself. I've been catching up with friends.

15 June

Mum's back at work. It's such a big boost for her. She has her life back. I feel like I can get my life back, too.

17 June

I start work in a shop in two weeks. It's temporary, just for the summer. It's minimum wage but it's my wage!

7 July

Mum's got a date! Her boss asked her out! Go, Mum. You've still got it!

14 July

Going to a music festival this weekend with people from college. Mum is fine about being on her own – she might be seeing her boss again.

17 July

The festival was great – apart from the mud and only one toilet for every 10,000 people!

26 July

Work is dull. I make sandwiches and sell pies all day. On the other hand, it's money in my pocket. Just over a month till college starts again.

18 August

Mum has cancer again. She woke up with a pain in her hip. Cancer has made the bone so weak it broke when she lay on it. I spent the whole day at the hospital. The doctors kept her asleep while they did tests. That's good. She would be so scared now.

21 August

Mum's dying. There's no cure for the cancer. It has spread all through her body. How can it have happened again so quickly? She's not going to get better. They don't know how long she has, and all they can do now is make sure she isn't in pain. They told us yesterday. I tried to write in the diary last night but I just couldn't.

23 August

Aunt Fiona arrived this morning. She drove through the night. She had a shower and we went to the hospital. Mum was asleep when we got there. The doctor said Mum has a year at the most. Aunt Fiona kept it together until we got home. I can hear her crying now.

25 August

I'm supposed to start college next week. I need to study or I won't get to university, but how can I think about studying when Mum is dying?

28 August

When Mum gets out of hospital she'll need someone to look after her. Mum and Aunt Fiona say I have to go on with my education. They think I should go and live with Aunt Fiona in Edinburgh and finish studying up there. They want me to think about it for a few days.

29 August

I've decided. I'm not leaving Mum. I'm staying here.

31 August

I had to meet a nurse today to talk about how hard it will be to look after Mum every day. I did a lot of this stuff earlier this year when Mum was ill, but it's going to be even harder than before.

3 September

It turns out there is support for carers. There are organisations that help. I have their phone numbers and links.

5 September

Mum is going to be in hospital for a few more days at least. Aunt Fiona took me to college. I saw Miss Afzal. She was sympathetic. I have to tell her what's happening and we'll work it out as we go along. I don't think I'm going to be at college much this year. I can't study and look after Mum. I have to choose between my future and my mum. Mum wins every time.

7 September

We brought Mum's bed downstairs so it's in the living room.

9 September

Mum is home. They brought her home by ambulance. She hated the fuss.

11 September

Aunt Fiona went home today. She has a business to run and she can't do it from here. She'll be back soon.

14 September

Mum is in pain all the time but she doesn't want to take the really strong pills she has. I hate seeing her like this. It's like she's given up. Being stuck in bed is making it much worse.

15 September

Mum's boss came to see her today. She didn't want to see him. She didn't want to see me either.

17 September

Mum broke down today. She cried and kept saying she was sorry for ruining my life. She has cancer but she's more worried that I'm missing college! The guilt is really hurting her and I don't know how to help.

18 September

Aunt Fiona arrived this morning. I escaped for a few hours and met Miss Afzal for a coffee. She suggested I take this year out and finish college next year. Mum's not going to get better. The only way I can start again next year is if Mum is gone. I can't think about that.

20 September

Mum got out of bed today. We had to help her, but she was able to go to the loo properly. She's been embarrassed that we have had to help her with that. It's been horrible for me, too.

21 September

I hate it when Aunt Fiona goes home. When she's here I don't feel like everything is on my shoulders. I sound so selfish.

22 September

We have a wheelchair. Mum can move herself around the house in it.

23 September

I found Mum in the garden. She got her wheelchair out of the back door. We sat and caught the sun. She remembered me playing in the garden with Dad. She hardly ever talks about Dad. She didn't actually say it, but it was like she thought they'd be together again soon.

28 September

We went to the corner shop. Some people were really nice. Others were just weird, as if they didn't know what to say or they were scared of catching something.

3 October

We had another shopping trip. This time we went to the supermarket. Mum bought all of our favourite things. She said she wants to make tea tomorrow.

4 October

Mum didn't make tea today. She showed me how to cook one of my favourites meals. We hadn't done anything like that since I was tiny.

6 October

We watched Dirty Dancing tonight. I got up on Mum's bed beside her. We used to watch it all the time when I was a kid.

8 October

Mum's reading *Pride and Prejudice*. We've been talking about it. It's nice.

11 October

Mum's doing all her favourite things. She's reading her favourite books, watching her favourite films and TV shows, and cooking the things I like most. She's doing all the things she has loved most and she's sharing them with me.

16 October

I met David when I was doing some shopping. He was with a bunch of people from college. He asked how I was and asked about Mum. One of the girls from college was staring daggers at me. I think she has her eye on David. I can't think about that just now.

18 October

Mum's boss came to visit today. She saw him this time. While he was with Mum, I phoned one of the support groups. It's hard to stay cheerful for her all the time. I just needed to talk to someone.

21 October

Mum's in hospital again. I heard her fall and found her lying beside her bed.

24 October

Mum's cancer has spread. It's affecting different parts of her body. It's why she has a fever and collapsed. The doctors are trying to make her stable.

26 October

I should have been with Mum to stop her falling.
I know I can't be with her every minute. It still
feels like it's my fault.

2 November

The doctors want Mum to go to a place where
they can watch her all the time. They call it a
hospice. Mum wants to be at home. I think she
should go to the hospice. Doctors and nurses can
look after her better than I can. I need to talk to
Aunt Fiona.

5 November

Mum's really angry with me for agreeing to send
her to the hospice. She wanted to come home.
She doesn't think she'll ever get home.

8 November

Mum moved to a hospice today. It's closer to
home than the hospital. She's still angry. She's not
talking to me.

11 November

Mum asked for her laptop, some DVDs and some books. She's still not happy but at least she's talking.

13 November

I've got nothing to do. The hospice only lets me visit for a few hours each day. For the rest of the time I have nothing to do.

14 November

I tried planning what I will do next year. I don't want to think that far ahead.

15 November

I'm spending too much time alone. I texted David for the first time in months. He's too busy to meet up.

21 November

I'm going to think about Christmas. I'll make it as great as I can for Mum.

24 November

Aunt Fiona will be here for Christmas. We'll cook a proper dinner and take it to the hospice. I'm glad I have something to focus on.

29 November

Mum has a fever again. She's been moved from the hospice to hospital. Aunt Fiona is on her way.

30 November

Mum is worse. I don't think she has the strength to fight this.

3 December

Mum was awake for a while today. She wasn't strong enough to speak. I told her I love her before she went back to sleep. I'm sure she smiled.

5 December

We're going back to the hospital. They said we should be ready for the worst.

7 December

Mum died this morning. She didn't wake up again. We stayed with her for the past two days. She just sort of slipped away. It was peaceful, not sudden. I keep telling myself it's best for her. She's not in pain any more.

9 December

We arranged the funeral today. Mum wasn't religious, so we're not having hymns or a priest. Aunt Fiona called it a 'humanist service'. Mum's favourite music and people talking about her. I'm going to live with Aunt Fiona in Edinburgh after the funeral.

10 December

I had coffee with David today. I can't remember what we talked about. The cheerful Christmas music in the café didn't help. I didn't stay long.

13 December

It was the funeral today. The woman who talked
– the celebrant, they called her – was really
good. She made me smile as well as cry. A lot
of people came. They were all sympathetic and
kind. I don't know why but that made it worse. I
can't stand thinking of Mum in that coffin when
it went through the curtains out of sight at the
crematorium.

17 December

We finished packing everything into boxes. My life
is in boxes. I don't recognise the house anymore.
It's empty. The life and love are all gone.

25 December

This isn't Christmas. We tried. Aunt Fiona and
me. We have the tree, the turkey, the presents.
It just doesn't feel right. We gave up, switched
the tree's lights off and just ate on the settee. We
didn't open any presents. This hurts so much.

27 December

Aunt Fiona decided we needed to open the presents Mum left us. She got these when she knew she was dying. Aunt Fiona got a picture of the three of us, all happy and smiling. There were two for me. A big chunky sweater. 'Because it's cold in Edinburgh,' according to the tag. The other present is another diary. Mum had written on the inside. Her handwriting was so shaky. She'd put, 'Write about all the amazing things you will do in the next year. Write them and I will read them.' I didn't think I could miss her even more but I do.

29 December

We got on with life today. We bought some heavy clothes for me. Mum was right. Edinburgh really can get cold. There was some snow overnight

31 December

We're not doing New Year. It's ten o'clock and Aunt Fiona is already in bed. I'm going to bed as well after I finish this. We drove out to the coast this afternoon. It's a place Mum and Aunt Fiona used to go. It was cold but it stayed dry. The wind was pushing clouds through the sky towards us. It was one of Mum's favourite places. It was a place to say goodbye to a horrible year. Mum stays with us in our thoughts but we have to say goodbye to the sadness and remember the good times. Tomorrow we try to focus on the good memories. Tomorrow I write in my new diary.

ABOUT THE AUTHOR

Iain McLaughlin lives in his hometown of Dundee in Scotland, in a house filled with books. He has written more than a dozen novels and around 50 radio and audio plays, many based around popular characters and series including James Bond, Sherlock Holmes and *Doctor Who*. For a time, he was the editor of *The Beano* comic.